UP CLOSE™

DINOSAURS

HEATHER AMERY

PowerKiDS
press™

New York

Published in 2007 by The Rosen Publishing Group, Inc.
29 East 21st Street, New York, NY 10010

Copyright © 2007 Arcturus Publishing Limited

Author: Heather Amery
Editor (new edition): Ella Fern
Designers (new edition): Steve West, Steve Flight

Picture credits: Ardea: 5 top, 15 top, 17, 18 top; Discovery
Communications Inc: 16, 19; Natural History Museum (London): front
and back cover, title page, 2, 3, 4, 5 bottom, 6, 7, 8 top, bottom, 9, 10,
11 top, 12, 13 top, bottom, 14, 15 bottom, 20, 21, 23; Science Photo
Library: 11 bottom, 18 bottom.

Library of Congress Cataloging-in-Publication Data

Amery, Heather.
 Dinosaurs / Heather Amery.
    p. cm. -- (Up close)
 Includes bibliographical references and index.
 ISBN-13: 978-1-4042-3759-9 (lib. bdg.)
 ISBN-10: 1-4042-3759-3 (lib. bdg.)

1. Dinosaurs--Juvenile literat re. I. Title.
 QE861.5.A44 2007
 567.9--dc22

                              2006032998

Manufactured in China

CONTENTS

Millions and millions of years before any people lived on Earth, the world belonged to the dinosaurs! These amazing creatures first appeared about 228 million years ago (**mya** for short). Though their name means "terrible lizard," these prehistoric reptiles were not actually lizards, and many were not particularly terrible (unless you were a plant!). Some were as small as a chicken; others were longer than three buses in a row. From the knee-high to the sky-high, dinosaurs ruled the Earth for about 160 million years. Humans have only been around for about 1.5 million years, so we have a lot of catching up to do!

DINOSAUR DAYS

Dinosaurs lived during the Mesozoic Era, which began 245 mya and ended 65 mya. Each of three periods in the Mesozoic Era had its own cool creatures. The Triassic Period (248–206 mya) gave us the earliest dinosaurs, like *Herrerasaurus* (eh-ray-rah-SORE-us), as well as the first small mammals. The Jurassic Period (206–142 mya) produced plant-eaters like *Stegosaurus* (STEG-oh-SORE-us) and meat-eaters like *Allosaurus* (al-oh-SORE-us). And the Cretaceous Period (142–65 mya) was the time of *Triceratops* (try-SER-a-tops), *lower right,* and *Deinonychus* (die-NON-i-kus)—and, sadly, the end of the line for the dinosaurs.

EMPTY NESTERS

Like most reptiles, dinosaurs laid and hatched from eggs. For many years, paleontologists (scientists who study prehistoric life) thought that dinosaurs were pretty relaxed parents, to put it mildly: in their tough neighborhood, maybe self-preservation was considered a higher priority than taking care of the kids! But some fossils now indicate that certain dinosaurs may have been very protective of their young, like one Cretaceous plant-eater who apparently guarded its babies and brought them food. Paleontologists named this dinosaur *Maiasaura* (MY-ah-SORE-ah), or "good mother lizard." Thanks, mom!

DOMINATED

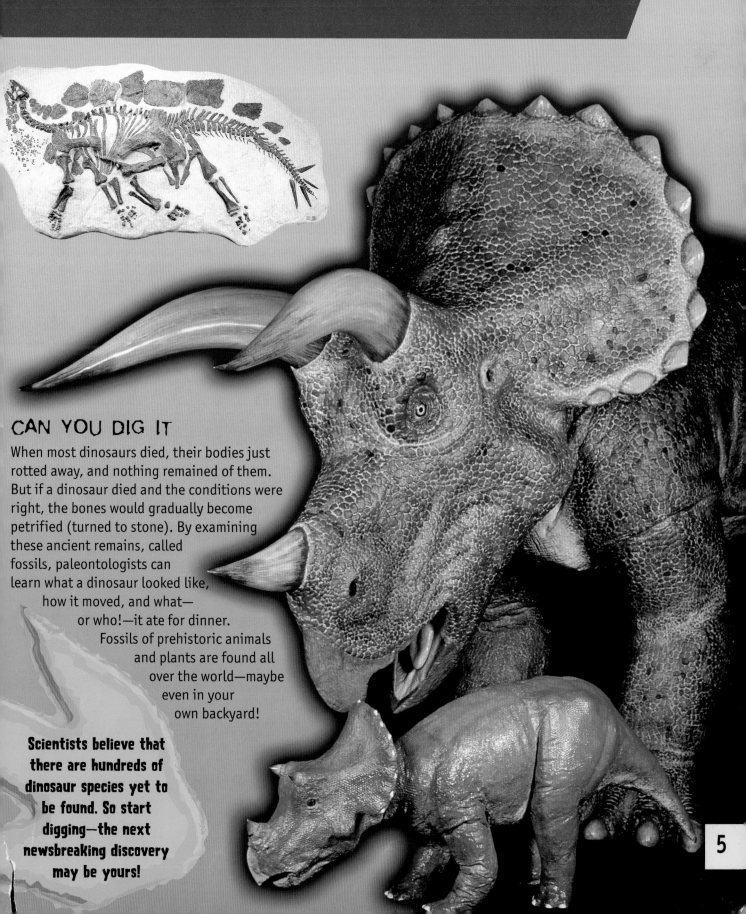

CAN YOU DIG IT

When most dinosaurs died, their bodies just rotted away, and nothing remained of them. But if a dinosaur died and the conditions were right, the bones would gradually become petrified (turned to stone). By examining these ancient remains, called fossils, paleontologists can learn what a dinosaur looked like, how it moved, and what— or who!—it ate for dinner. Fossils of prehistoric animals and plants are found all over the world—maybe even in your own backyard!

Scientists believe that there are hundreds of dinosaur species yet to be found. So start digging—the next newsbreaking discovery may be yours!

Mighty Meat-

Carnivorous dinosaurs, the most fearsome, wouldn't have won any popularity contests. Some, like the recently discovered **Giganotosaurus** (JI-gah-NO-tuh-SORE-us), were humungous, but there were also mini meat-munchers like **Compsognathus** (komp-soh-NAY-thus), which was no bigger than a modern chicken. But they all had the same favorite meal—MEAT—and the tools to get it. When their dagger-like, flesh-ripping teeth fell or wore out, new ones grew in to take their place. No dentures for these dudes!

Paleontologists can learn what dinosaurs ate by examining fossils called coprolites—the scientific name for dino dung.

RUN FOR YOUR LIFE!

Some of the most dangerous carnivorous dinosaurs were small but speedy—and well-armed! *Deinonychus* was only 10 feet (3 m) long, but fast and fierce. Its name, which means "terrible claw," refers to the long, curved claw on each of its back feet, which it used to slash its prey. It also had a relatively big brain—bad news for its intended victims.

Eaters

ARMED AND DANGEROUS

At 35 feet (11 m) long, *Allosaurus* was the top predator of the Jurassic Period. It had a powerful tail, three strong claws on each hand, and a mouthful of teeth with jagged edges perfect for tearing and chewing flesh. You wouldn't hear this diner complain that his meat was too tough!

The great meat-eater *Megalosaurus* (MEG-ah-loh-SORE-us), or "great reptile," was the first dinosaur ever to be named. When its leg bone was unearthed, people first thought they had discovered the remains of a giant man. Not quite!

FOOD FIGHTS

While some herbivorous (plant-eating) dinosaurs may have been gentle, they didn't necessarily give up without a struggle. In Mongolia's Gobi Desert, the bones of a meat-eating *Velociraptor* (vel-O-si-RAP-tor, meaning "speedy robber") and the bones of a plant-eating *Protoceratops* (pro-toe-SER-a-tops) were found together, indicating a fight to the finish—for both of them. So much for fast food!

Herbivores: Gentle Giants?

The biggest creatures that have ever walked the Earth were the herbivorous (plant-eating) dinosaurs. The neck alone of the **Mamenchisaurus** (mah-MEN-chee-SORE-us) measured 36 feet (11 m) long—the length of a school bus. Another long-neck, **Seismosaurus** (SIZE-moh-SORE-us), may have measured nearly 130 feet (40 m). That's the length of two bowling alley lanes! The plant-eaters went looking for food, not trouble, so other dinosaurs had little to fear from them. But a meat-eater that provoked or attacked them might get more than it bargained for. The three facial horns and neck shield of **Triceratops** made it hard for a carnivore to get in a good chomp. And **Ankylosaurus** (an-KIE-loh-SORE-us) had a rock-hard ball at the end of its tail to club any attackers. Talk about mean cuisine!

VEGETARIAN VENGEANCE

Imagine long-necked reptiles the height of six men standing on each other's shoulders, and as heavy as a dozen elephants! *Brachiosaurus* (brak-ee-oh-SORE-us) was way too massive to move fast. But it had a thick and powerful tail, great for whacking Jurassic attackers like *Allosaurus* and *Ceratosaurus* (seh-rat-oh-SORE-us). And while its thick, tree-like limbs weren't built for speed, "Big Brac" might have been able to rear back on its hind legs and crash its front ones down on its enemy. Take that!

WEAPONS OR WEATHERPROOFING?

The strange-looking *Stegosaurus* has long puzzled paleontologists. Most now agree that its triangular plates formed a row down its back and served as a sort of prehistoric furnace *and* air-conditioner. *Stegosaurus* may have turned its plates to face the sun to soak in rays and warm its body, while a breeze through the plates would cool it down. Scientists used to think that the plates discouraged predators from snacking on *Stegosaurus*, but further study has revealed that they weren't really too sturdy. Fortunately, the 3 foot (1 m)-long, spear-like spikes on its tail would have been excellent weapons.

Poor *Stegosaurus* has another claim to fame besides its weird appearance: its walnut-sized brain was smaller than any other dinosaur's.

The polished pebbles found among some plant-eating dinosaur remains suggest that before they gulped down their leafy lunches, some plant-eaters may have swallowed stones to help grind up the food in their stomachs, like some birds do today.

TOUGH LOVE

The plant-eating *Pachycephalosaurus* (PAK-ee-SEF-a-loh-SORE-us) was a real bonehead! The solid dome on the top of its skull was 10 inches (25 cm) thick. Some scientists believe that during mating season, rival males would fight for females by charging at each other headfirst. Those built-in crash helmets sure came in handy.

BACK OFF!

This dinosaur, the *Triceratops*, looks a bit like a modern-day rhinoceros. Since it was a strict vegetarian, its three horns were not used for hunting, but for defense against hungry predators. The horns might also have been used in mating displays, and in fights between males competing for the attention of a female. *Triceratops* used its huge mouth and jaw to chomp through tough plants. Its huge appetite meant it had to stay on the move to find enough to eat.

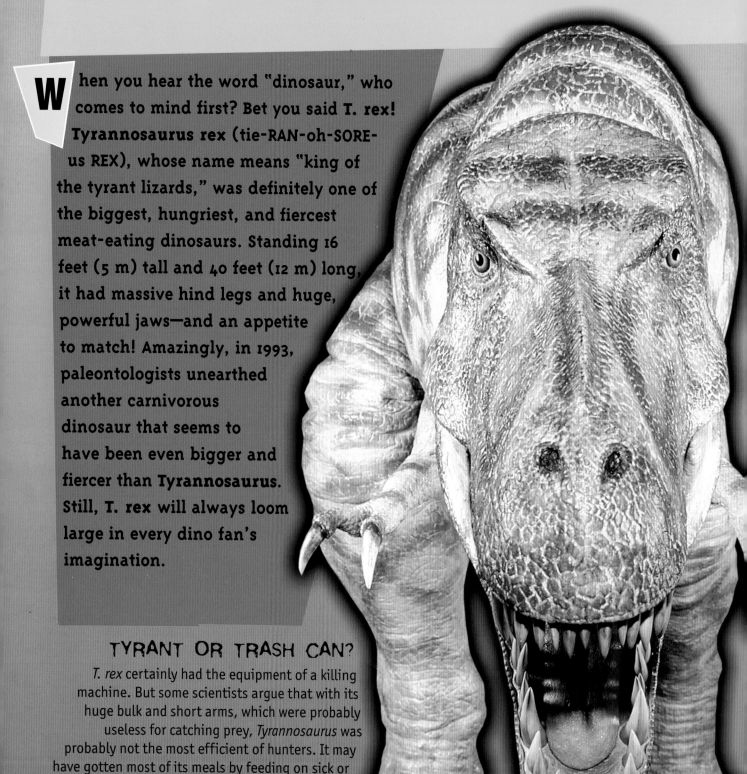

Tyrannosaurus:

When you hear the word "dinosaur," who comes to mind first? Bet you said **T. rex!** **Tyrannosaurus rex** (tie-RAN-oh-SORE-us REX), whose name means "king of the tyrant lizards," was definitely one of the biggest, hungriest, and fiercest meat-eating dinosaurs. Standing 16 feet (5 m) tall and 40 feet (12 m) long, it had massive hind legs and huge, powerful jaws—and an appetite to match! Amazingly, in 1993, paleontologists unearthed another carnivorous dinosaur that seems to have been even bigger and fiercer than **Tyrannosaurus.** Still, **T. rex** will always loom large in every dino fan's imagination.

TYRANT OR TRASH CAN?

T. rex certainly had the equipment of a killing machine. But some scientists argue that with its huge bulk and short arms, which were probably useless for catching prey, *Tyrannosaurus* was probably not the most efficient of hunters. It may have gotten most of its meals by feeding on sick or wounded dinosaurs—or even by eating the remains of prey killed by other carnivores. Imagine: a king eating leftovers!

THE Ex-REX?

T. rex's arms were so short that they couldn't even touch each other. No applause from those claws!

ALL THE BETTER TO EAT YOU WITH

Tyrannosaurus rex was some bigmouth! With a head as long as a refrigerator, it could have opened its jaws wide enough to swallow a man in one gulp. Curved, jagged teeth, longer than a human's hand, could puncture its prey's organs before tearing it apart. *T. rex*'s teeth were made for ripping, not chewing, so it had to swallow each mouthful whole. What lousy table manners!

SUPER-REX

In 1990, one of the largest and most complete *Tyrannosaurus* skeletons ever unearthed was found in South Dakota. Named "Sue," after its discoverer, this fossilized dinosaur was one tough customer. A number of its bones had been broken but had rehealed over time. The broken bones were probably a result of fierce battles with other *T. rex*.

THE RIGHTFUL KING

Giganotosaurus, whose name means "giant lizard of the south," was discovered in Argentina in 1993. When this dinosaur's skull and thigh bone measured bigger than Sue's, it became clear that *Tyrannosaurus* was *rex* no more! How long will *Giganotosaurus* be #1? Its reign could end at any time, since new types of dinosaurs are being found every year. But until then—Long Live the King!

The Real Sea

While dinosaurs roamed the Earth, equally awesome beasts ruled the seas. Many of these oceanic monsters evolved from land reptiles and adapted to life in the water. But though some looked pretty fishy, they were still reptiles, and had to come to the water's surface to breathe between dives, like whales and dolphins do. The prehistoric sea monsters came in all shapes and sizes. Some had long necks and flippers, while others had long jaws filled with razor-sharp teeth. One of the biggest, **Kronosaurus (KRON-oh-SORE-us)**, with its eight-foot head, feasted on prehistoric squids, sharks—and its fellow seafaring reptiles!

MONSTER OR MYTH?

Sea monster sightings have been reported all over the world. The most famous of these creatures is Scotland's "Nessie," the so-called Loch Ness Monster. Descriptions of Nessie—and a photo that turned out to be a fake—made it sound like a water-going dinosaur. Few people believe there are any such monsters today ... but never say never!

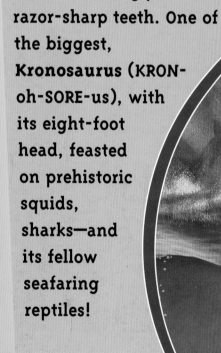

MONSTERS

Beautifully preserved fossils suggest that *Ichthyosaurs* didn't lay eggs but gave birth to their little ones live in the water.

GONE FISHIN'

Ichthyosaurs (IKH-thee-oh-sores), like this 49-foot (15 m)-long *Shonisaurus* (shon-ee-SORE-us), were the super swimmers of the prehistoric seas. They looked and lived a lot like modern-day dolphins—but they were much, *much* bigger. With their sleek bodies, back fins, and strong tails, the *Ichthyosaurs* zipped through the water as fast as 25 miles per hour (40 km/h). When their big eyes spotted a tasty meal, their long, tooth-lined jaws would open and *snap!* Fish du jour!

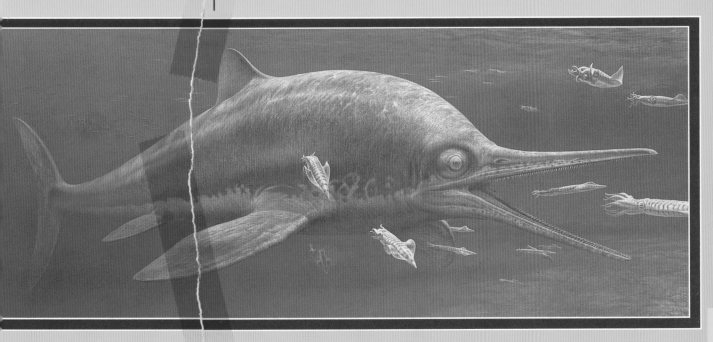

DOWN IN THE DEPTHS

With their skinny necks and roly-poly bodies, *Plesiosaurs* (PLE-see-oh-sores) may have looked awkward, but did just fine as fishermen, thanks to paddle-like flippers that let them twist and turn. To help themselves sink, they sometimes swallowed rocks to act as ballast. Now there's an appetizer that would fill anyone up!

Fearsome Fliers

In prehistoric times, reptiles not only ruled the Earth and seas but also filled the skies. The **Pterosaurs** (Teh-ruh-SORES), flying reptiles with wings made of skin, fed on creatures from both land and sea. Some were as tiny as a sparrow, but others had a wingspan the size of a small airplane's—along with knife-sharp teeth. Look out below!

SUPER SCOOPER

Pteranodon (Ter-RANN-oh-don) was one funny-looking fisherman. Its head had a pointy crest and even pointier jaws. *Pteranodon* would skim through the water, scoop up fish, and swallow them whole—the same handy method used by pelicans today.

FINALLY ... FEATHERS!

Archeopteryx (ark-ee-OP-ter-iks), which means "ancient wing," is the first flying reptile known to have had feathery wings. But don't let the feathers fool you—this was no ordinary bird. Its fossils reveal a skeleton of a reptile with dinosaur-like teeth and claws on its wings, which it may have used to climb trees. Some scientists think it may have been more of a glider than a flier— okay at catching a breeze, but lousy at takeoffs!

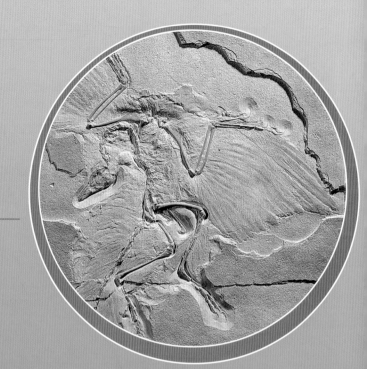

Quetzalcoatlus (kwet-zal-co-AT-lus) was the largest creature ever to sail the skies. And sail or glide on air currents is what it probably did; its enormous wings may have been too big to flap! With wings up to 40 feet across, this pterosaur was the size of a two-seater airplane.

WINGING IT

At about 20 inches (51 cm) long, *Microraptor* [MY-cro-RAP-tor] was not big in dinosaur terms. Like *Archeopteryx*, it was covered in a thin layer of feathers. It also had four wings—two at the front, and two feathery back legs which it could use to help glide through the air. As if this weren't enough, a specially evolved feather at the end of its tail helped to it to balance and steer.

AIR-VOLUTION

Rhamphorynchus (RAM-foh-RING-khus), one of the
early pterosaurs, had spiky teeth great for spearing
fish. It also had a long, kite-like tail that may have
helped it steer through the skies. Later flying reptiles
like *Quetzalcoatlus* looked quite different, with much
shorter tails but longer necks.

The dinosaurs (and their airborne and seafaring relatives) ruled for 165 million years. But 65 mya, they all disappeared. What's the deal? Did something kill them all at once, or did they gradually become extinct over a year ... a decade ... a millennium? Did one catastrophic event wipe out prehistoric life, or did a combination of factors cause this disappearing act? There are several theories that try to answer these questions. But until someone invents a time machine to take us back to the dinosaur days, we may never know exactly what happened to these awesome beasts.

VIOLENT VOLCANOES

One theory blames the dinosaurs' disappearance on huge volcanoes in what is now India. These volcanoes erupted late in the Cretaceous Period, and may have spewed so much lava, volcanic ash, and poisonous gas into the air that the dinosaurs couldn't survive the climate change. Just another example of the dangers of secondhand smoke.

Disappear

LIGHTS OUT

At the end of the Cretaceous Period, a massive meteorite—more than 6 miles (10 km) wide—may have crashed down on Earth. Many scientists think that the huge clouds of dust from this collision blocked out the sun for weeks or maybe even months. So much for that savage tan! Plenty of small animals (such as mammals, birds, and insects) survived this big bang. But no sun was no fun for the dominant reptiles, who would have frozen to death, starved to death (since many plants died without sunlight), or both.

BABY, IT'S COLD OUTSIDE

A less dramatic explanation of extinction is that Earth's climate changed gradually, and the creatures that lived there changed with it. Once warm and tropical, our planet's weather got drier and cooler, which was fine for some creatures but devastating for dinosaurs, who couldn't handle the big chill.

Believe it or not, here are some of the wackier suggestions about what happened to the dinosaurs:

They ate all the plants and starved to death.

Rat-sized mammals ate all their eggs.

Space aliens carried them away. (Gee ... maybe there are *Velociraptors* on Venus and a *Maiasaura* on Mars!)

What do you think?

Glossary

Ballast (BA-lust)
Heavy material used to stabilize a boat in the water.

Carnivore (KAR-neh-vor)
An animal that eats meat.

Cretaceous Period
(krih-TAY-shus PIR-ee-ud)
The third and final period of the Mesozoic era
(142–65 million years ago).

Fossil (FAH-sul)
The mold or impression of an ancient plant or animal
that is preserved in mineral deposits.

Herbivore (ER-buh-vor)
An animal that eats plants.

Ichthyosaurs (IK-thee-eh-sorz)
Large reptiles with fins who lived in the sea during the
Mesozoic era.

Jurassic Period (ju-RA-sik PIR-ee-ud)
The second period of the Mesozoic era
(206–142 million years ago).

Lava (LAH-vuh)
Magma that rises out of the Earth's crust and flows out
of volcanoes in eruption.

Mesozoic Era (meh-zuh-ZOH-ik ER-uh)
Geological period that began 245 million years ago and
ended 65 million years ago.

Meteorite (MEE-tee-uh-ryt)
A rock or metal object from space that has collided with
the Earth.

Millenium (muh-LEH-nee-um)
A period of one thousand years.

Oceanic (OH-shee-a-nik)
Belonging to, or living in, the ocean.

Paleontologist (pay-lee-on-TAH-luh-jist)
Someone who studies fossils.

Plesiosaurs (PLEE-see-uh-sorz)
Thin-bodied reptiles with flippers who lived in the sea
during the Mesozoic era.

Predator (PREH-duh-tur)
An animal (a carnivore) that hunts and eats other animals.

Prehistoric (pree-his-TOR-ik)
From the time before recorded history began.

Pterosaurs (TER-uh-sorz)
Flying reptiles from the Mesozoic era.

Reptile (REP-tyl)
A cold-blooded vertebrate (animal with a backbone),
covered in scales or a horny plate. Reptiles include
lizards, snakes, crocodiles and turtles.

Triassic Period (try-A-sik PIR-ee-ud)
The earliest period of the Mesozoic era
(248–206 million years ago).

Volcanic ash (vol-KA-nik ASH)
Particles of burnt lava that erupt out of volcanoes.

Further Reading

Dinosaur
John Malam, Dorling Kindersley (Experience series), 2006

Dinosaur (Ultimate Sticker Book)
Dorling Kindersley, 2004

Dinosaurs
Stephanie Turnbull, Usborne (Beginners series), 2003

Dinosaurs! The Biggest Baddest Strangest Fastest
Howard Zimmerman, Atheneum, 2000

The Ultimate Book of Dinosaurs
Dougal Dixon, Ticktock Publishing, 2005

WEB SITES

Due to the changing nature of Internet links, PowerKids Press has developed an online list of Web sites related to this book. This site is updated regularly. Please use this link to access the list:
www.powerkidslinks.com/CCR/dino/

Index

A
Allosaurus *4, 7, 9*
Ankylosaurus *9*
Archeopteryx *18*
Argentina *13*

B
Brachiosaurus *9*

C
carnivores *6–8, 9, 12, 22*
Ceratosaurus *9*
claws *6, 13, 18*
Compsognathus *6*
Cretaceous era *4, 20, 21, 22*

D
Deinonychus *4, 6*

E
extinction *20–21*

F
feathers *18*
fins *15*
flippers *14, 15, 16*
fossils *4, 5, 6, 13, 15, 18, 22*

G
Giganotosaurus *6, 13*

H
herbivores *8, 9–11, 22*
Herrerasaurus *4*
horns *9, 11*

I
Ichthyosaurs *15, 22*

J
jaws *11, 13, 14, 15, 17*
Jurassic era *4, 7, 9, 22*

K
Kronosaurus *14*

L
lizard *4, 12*
Loch Ness Monster *14*

M
Maiasaura *4, 21*
Mamenchisaurus *9*
mating rituals *11*
Megalosaurus *7*
Mesozoic era *4, 22*
Meteorite *21, 22*
Microraptor *18*
Mongolia *8*

P
Pachycephalosaurus *11*
paleontologists *4, 5, 6, 10, 12, 22*
plesiosaurs *16, 22*
predators *6–8, 10, 11, 22*
prey *6, 12, 13*
Protoceratops *8*
Pteranodon *17*
Pterosaurs *17–19, 22*

Q
Quetzalcoatlus *18, 19*

R
reptiles *4, 7, 9, 14, 19, 21, 22*
  flying reptiles *17–19*
Rhamphorynchus *19*

S
Seismosaurus *9*
sharks *14*
Shonisaurus *15*
skeletons *13, 18*
South Dakota *13*
squid *14*
Stegosaurus *4, 10*
swimming *14–16*

T
tails *7, 9, 10, 15, 19*
teeth *6, 7, 13, 14, 17, 18, 19*
Triassic era *4, 22*
Triceratops *4, 9, 11*
Tyrannosaurus Rex *12–13*

V
Velociraptor *8, 21*
volcanoes *20*

W
weather *21*
wings *17, 18*